Tracing Your Cherokee Roots

Updated Edition

Joseph Robert Reece

DEDICATION

This book is dedicated to all those individuals looking to find their Cherokee roots. I wish you the best in your journey.

CONTENTS

ACKNOWLEDGMENTS

I want to acknowledge my wife Barbie for sticking by my side and being supportive in all my ventures. All the writing, the research, it all takes time, and she has been patient, understanding, and supportive during the writing of this book and the countless hours spent when I was tracing my family history. I also want to acknowledge my children Tyson and Amelia and the love and support they've both shown me throughout all that I do. Finally, I want to acknowledge all my family and friends and everyone who has supported me in the past, present, and future. I have nothing but love for you.

Introduction

There are many Americans who have the story of their Cherokee relative who hid their Native American ancestry for fear of persecution. Due to historical wrongs such as the Trail of Tears, the Lakota 38 mass execution, the boarding schools, the smallpox blankets, and many other tragedies Native Americans were forced to endure it would be no wonder why some Cherokees would choose to lie about their Ancestry.

First contact with Europeans happened relatively early as compared to other tribes in 1540 when Spanish explorer Hernando DeSoto arrived in historic Cherokee Nation. Trade and intermarriage followed soon after. With American Independence still hundreds of years away U.S. census rolls weren't even a pipe dream yet.

Tracing your Cherokee Ancestor back to this time may not be possible as written records weren't quite flourishing yet, and if they left the tribe finding any record of it just might not exist.

Genetic testing doesn't go back that far either as with each generation the DNA from your Ancestor is cut in half. In 5 generations or around 100 years there would be only 3% of that Ancestor still with you and after another 100 years it'd be less than 0.1%.

If the Ancestor you seek to discover is more recent, then tracing their information is much more possible to find and this book can be used as a guide to help you discover more about them.

As of the publication of this book the Cherokee Nation is the largest tribe in the United States with over 400,000 enrolled citizens. The Navajo Nation enrollment numbers are a close second and had more enrolled citizens than the Cherokee Nation earlier this year.

Aside from the Cherokee Nation there are also the United Keetoowah Band (UKB) and the Eastern Band of Cherokee Indians. All three tribes have a shared common history and language and meet on a yearly basis for a tri-council meeting. Aside from the three federally recognized Cherokee tribes there are also state recognized Cherokee tribes, although their authenticity has been questioned and individuals who are of Cherokee descent, but are not enrolled either from not knowing how, not wanting to, and/or not being eligible to enroll.

History

The Cherokee Nation is where most Cherokees are enrolled. Prior to the Indian Removal Act also known as the Trail of Tears all Cherokees were one together. The original Cherokee Nation was massive and spanned over many East Coast and Southern modern-day states. From broken treaties, encroachment on lands, and other factors some Cherokees moved west prior to the Trail of Tears. These Cherokees settled in modern day Arkansas and Oklahoma area. These Cherokees were known as the Old Settlers and the United Keetoowah Band claims they are the descendants of the Old Settlers.

Many Cherokees did not move west voluntarily and even fought the Removal Act in the Supreme Court and won! But Andrew Jackson has been quoted as saying, "John Marshall has made his decision; now let him enforce it" before continuing to mark one of the gravest times in American history. Once these Cherokees arrived in Indian Territory they were met with the Old Settlers and together built a strong Tribal Nation. Schools, courts, jails, and everything else you'd expect from a government were built by Cherokees in their new homeland. Through dialog of tribal leaders such as Sequoyah and Jesse Bushyhead the Act of Union was made which united all Cherokees in the region.

A small group of Cherokees hid in the North Carolina hills and eventually moved to the Qualla Boundary. These Cherokees never left their homelands, and their descendants are the Eastern Band of Cherokee Indians.

In 1887 the U.S. government enacted the Dawes Act which took the promised land from the tribes in Indian Territory and allotted it to individual Indians. Any "excess" land was available to settlers during the land rush of 1889. Part of the Dawes Act was the Dawes Commission who interviewed Indians in the area and put them on what are known as the Dawes Rolls.

There were many issues with these interviews and rolls as some numbers were made up on the spot for blood quantum. For example, there are some individuals who are listed as 3/8 while their sibling was listed as full blood even though they shared the same parents. Some who were of mixed blood were put on the rolls as Freedman instead of Cherokee by Blood even though they were Cherokee. These issues weren't exclusive to Cherokees either as Choctaws, Chickasaws, Creeks, and Seminoles were all going through the same process too.

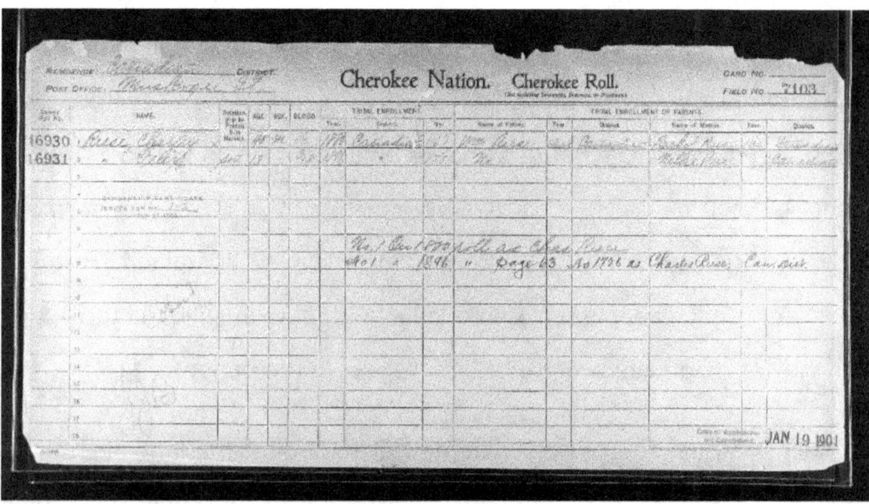

These imperfect rolls are now the basis for enrollment for both Cherokee Tribes in Oklahoma, the Cherokee Nation, and the United Keetoowah

Band. The enrollment requirements for the Cherokee Nation are to be descended from a Cherokee on the Dawes Roll or one of the adopted tribes such as Delaware with no minimum blood quantum requirement.

The United Keetoowah Band bases their enrollment on the 1949 UKB rolls and the Dawes Rolls. Although the UKB claims to have originated from the Old Settlers there is no requirement and many of their citizens are descended from those who walked the Trail of Tears. Aside from having an ancestor on one of the rolls they require least ¼ Cherokee blood quantum.

The Eastern Band of Cherokee Indians enrollment is based on the Baker Roll of 1924, and they require 1/16 of Eastern Cherokee blood to enroll.

Tracing Family History

Now that you understand some of the history behind the Cherokee tribes and their enrollment requirements you may have a better idea on where to look in your family tree for your Cherokee ancestors. The first thing you're going to want to do is make a family tree starting with yourself. You'll want names, birth dates, birth places, marriage dates, death dates, places of death, and any relevant information you can gather. The more information you know from your own records the easier the following steps will be.

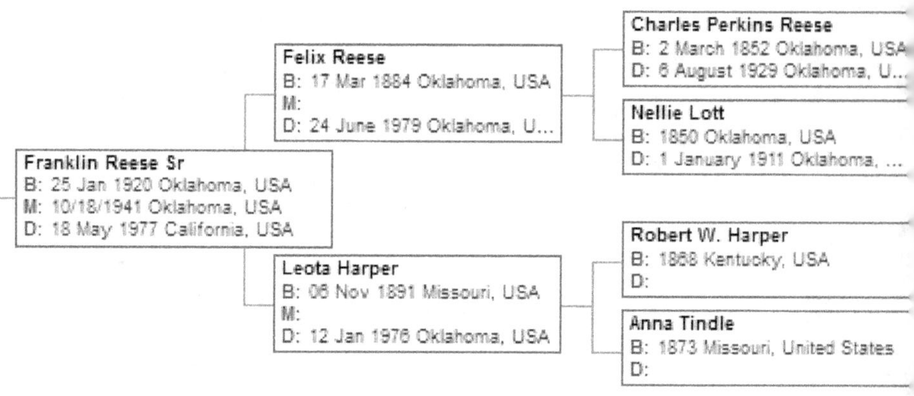

Sample Family Tree showing my great grandfather, his parents, and his grandparents.

Let's say you now have an incomplete family tree maybe going back as far as great grandparents. For some of you this may already be enough to determine if you're eligible for enrollment in one of the Cherokee tribes, for younger generations there is probably some more digging to do.

You'll want to start looking at census data from the furthest back you can trace. Censuses can give clues on who your great grandmother's parents were and where they may have lived. Military records such as any service records are also of great help. Ancestry.com is an amazing source of information as they have massive amounts of digital records. Through Ancestry you may also get lucky and one of your relatives may have already traced back and you may be able to see their tree. If you're not looking to spend any money the LDS Mormon church has their own genealogy website at familysearch.org

Another way of tracing genealogy is through birth and death certificates which you'll have to do anyways if you plan on enrolling. These certificates usually have important names and dates and most importantly they're legal documents which establish a legal connection to your ancestor. If obtaining birth/death certificates for enrollment purposes make sure you get it from the state and not the county. Similarly, to a family tree you'll want to know names, dates, and locations of the ancestor in question when requesting the certificate. If you don't have that information, it may be on their children's birth certificate. You may also have to establish the legal connection to that ancestor through birth and death certificates before you can order theirs. The downside to birth/death certificates is they only go back so far before there's not a record anymore.

Fortunately, Cherokees have kept records or have had records kept of them for hundreds of years. Prior to the Dawes Rolls there were others. If your ancestor is on one of these rolls, but not on the Dawes, Baker, and/or UKB rolls then you probably can't enroll as Cherokee, but at least you have bragging rights.

1949 – UKB Roll

1924 – Baker Roll (EBCI)

1909 – Guion Miller Roll (EBCI)

1908 – Churchill Roll (EBCI)

1898 – Dawes Roll

1883 – Hester Roll

1869 – Swetland Roll

1852 – Drennen Roll

1852 – Chapman Roll

1851 – Old Settler Roll

1851 – Siler Roll

1848 – Mullay Roll

1835 – Henderson Roll

1817 – Emigration Rolls

1814 – Muster Roll

These rolls are not absolute though as Cherokees have been in America long before 1814. There are also many instances where the tribe of your ancestor is different than you had originally thought. I thought I was

Apache for most of my life until I started looking into my family history. So, don't be surprised if you go looking to find one thing and discover something completely different than you expected.

If you're having trouble tracing your Cherokee ancestor(s) the Cherokee Nation offers help with genealogy at their research center in the Capital of the Cherokee Nation, Tahlequah. Downloadable forms can be found at VisitCherokeeNation.com

Enrollment Process

So, you've found your ancestor on the Dawes Roll (or another roll) and have copies of birth/death certificates tracing yourself to this ancestor, now what? For the Cherokee Nation the process is fairly straight forward. At Cherokee.org there is an enrollment packet that you can print and fill out. The first part of the process is obtaining your CDIB (certificate degree of Indian blood) or "white card" and some tribes call it a CIB.

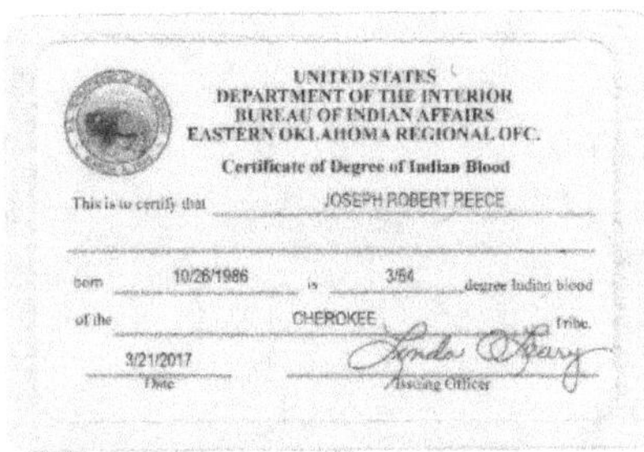

To get your CDIB you'll fill out the forms which is pretty much a family tree with some basic information about yourself. You'll include the birth/death certificates that trace you to your ancestor along with copies of I.D. and a sworn affidavit. The enrollment office gets a lot of inquiries and applications daily and at many times have a large back log so processing times can take quite a while sometimes.

The Cherokee Nation unlike some tribes process and issue CDIBs along with tribal IDs. It's important to note that CDIBs are documents from the Bureau of Indian Affairs (BIA) which is part of the Department of the Interior which is a U.S. Federal Government agency. The Cherokee Nation is able to issue these from a partnership with the BIA.

Once you've been issued a CDIB they will issue a "blue card" next which is proof citizenship in the Cherokee Nation.

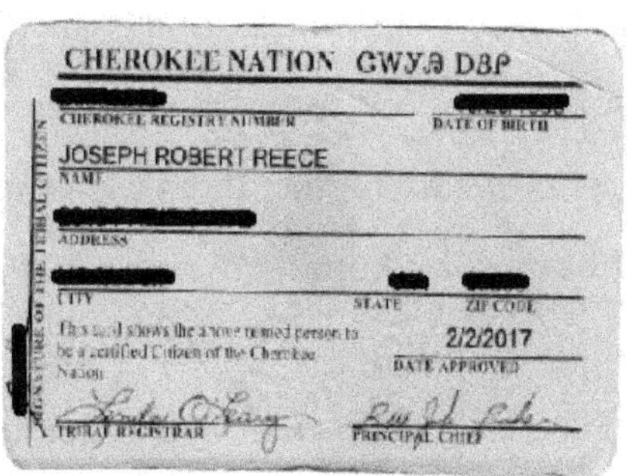

Both cards can be combined into one in a photo ID with a CDIB on the reverse side. One of the benefits of the photo ID is it is recognized as an approved form of ID from the federal government unlike some state IDs. This means it can be used when traveling and going through TSA airport security, entering the United States on ground from Mexico and/or Canada, and entering federal buildings that require ID.

Being a Citizen

Once you're a citizen of the Cherokee Nation or any Tribal Nation you'll have certain rights, responsibilities, and change in jurisdiction just like you would if you were a citizen of any other nation. Citizens of Germany have different laws that affect them than the citizens of France even though they're both in the European Union. It's much like that with citizens of Tribal Nations within the United States. Citizens of Tribal Nations hold dual citizenship with their Tribal Nation and the United States. Both Nations are Sovereign and separate but have certain obligations to each other established through treaties.

Each tribe has their own treaty rights, but there may be some commonality such as health and defense guarantees from the United States. Some treaty rights may include hunting and fishing in certain areas outside of the Tribal Nation boundaries. Other treaty rights include the Cherokee Nation's right to a Delegate to Congress. It's important to note that these treaties are the foundation from which the United States rests and are according to Article VI paragraph two of the U.S. Constitution the Supreme Law of the Land.

As a citizen of a Tribal Nation, it is your responsibility to protect and uphold these treaties just as it is the responsibility of citizens of the United States to uphold their obligations under treaty. Other responsibilities as a citizen are to uphold tribal laws, vote in tribal elections, and engage in civic duty to better your community.

Being a citizen of a Tribal Nation also means that the governing body which holds jurisdiction over your actions are fundamentally different than if you weren't an enrolled citizen. Laws and ordinances passed by your tribal council are binding and crimes committed within your Tribal Nation can lead to criminal arrest and sentencing (more of a reason to be a good citizen I guess). Child neglect, abuse, and adoption are also under the jurisdiction of your Tribal Nation and can lead to various proceedings under the authority of your Tribal Nation.

Unfortunately, these cases exist but you can help by participating in your civic duty by becoming a foster parent within your Tribal Nation. There is a need and you can be the change in your community.

Notable Cherokees

Dragging Canoe

Dragging Canoe was one of the last Cherokee War Chiefs. Dragging Canoe fought and led his forces during the Anglo-Cherokee War. Dragging Canoe has also been given credit as a role model for Tecumseh a well known Shawnee.

Ned Christie

Ned Christie was a Cherokee Statesmen who was wrongly accused of murder. His life was ended by a posse of U.S. Marshalls. Witnesses came forward after Christie's death about what had really happened the night of the murder.

Sequoyah

Possibly the most well known Cherokee, Sequoyah invented the Cherokee syllabary and laid the groundwork for a literate Cherokee Nation.

Wilma Mankiller

Wilma Mankiller was a modern Cherokee Chief who was known for her advancement of tribal sovereignty. She has even been featured on the reverse side of a U.S. quarter.

Notable Cherokees

John Ross

John Ross was Principle Chief of the Cherokee Nation during some of the most volatile times within the Cherokee Nation. During the Civil War Ross fled to D.C. to show the Cherokee allegiance to the Union.

Stand Watie

One of the most infamous Cherokees, Stand Watie sided with the Confederates during the Civil War. He was rumored to have done this due to a promise from the Confederates of allowing Cherokees to return to their homeland.

Notable Cherokees

Elias Boudinot

Elias Boudinot (previously Buck Watie) was the founder of the Cherokee Phoenix Newspaper and brother to Stand Watie. Both brothers mother was Susannah Charity Reese and were first cousins to my great x4 grandfather William "Wele" Reese.

Sam Starr

Sam Starr was an infamous outlaw who was the husband of Belle Starr shown above with Blue Duck. Belle Starr has been the subject of many outlaw movies with each portraying her and Sam in a different way. The Starr family were also related to the Watie family. Infamous bank robber Henry Starr was a grandchild of Sam Starr.

Other Tribes

As of January 2022, in the United States there are 574 federally recognized tribes. Each with their own history, culture, treaty rights, language, and many other aspects that make them their own sovereign entity. Each of these Tribal Nations also have their own enrollment requirements ranging in blood quantum requirements.

The "Five Civilized Tribes" (Cherokee, Choctaw, Chickasaw, Creek, and Seminole) all located in Oklahoma (although technically not in Oklahoma as they are Sovereign Nations) do not have a minimum blood quantum requirement and enrollment is based on descendants from the Dawes Roll. There are of course smaller bands of these tribes with different requirements.

Other tribes within Oklahoma include Apache, Comanche, Kickapoo, Osage, and many others. Their enrollment process is different than the Five Civilized Tribes, but there is more information on their websites.

If you're unsure of which tribe you may be from the first resource you should go to is your family. Ask questions, they may know more than you think about your family history. The older generations are going to have the most information, so talk to your elders.

DNA Testing

DNA tests can be helpful in many ways, but there should be a distinction between what they can and cannot do. A DNA test isn't currently accurate enough to tell you what tribe you're from or where that tribe is located. It can however help by checking to see if you have any DNA that matches other Native Americans. The percentages aren't always accurate and may not show any Native DNA if your ancestor was from too many generations ago.

On the opposite side of things you may have get a DNA result back that says you're 25% Native American, but that may be Native American from regions outside of the United States. Although Natives from the United States and the rest of the Americas are genetically similar the legal standing isn't the same. Simply having Native DNA does not entitle someone to citizenship within a Tribal Nation. Similar to having German DNA doesn't make you a German citizen.

DNA testing is also a great resource for finding other relatives who may having a better understanding of your shared family tree. You may match with a distant cousin who has a wealth of information that could be connected to your tribe.

It's also important to note that not all DNA testing companies use the same algorithms, so you may see different results from different companies. The results you receive depend on the sample population that the DNA company took testing from.

Results may also depend on what part of the genome is being sequenced. Even within a single company depending on the date a DNA test was conducted could depend on what part of the genome was sequenced and this could affect the ethnicity results.

Also, beware of scams as there are companies out there that guarantee they'll find Native DNA and follow this with some type of certificate. These scams have been caught in Canada and they'll even issue fake tribal ID cards. Individuals with the fake tribal ID cards will then try to use them as legitimate tribal ID cards and could face legal repercussions.

The U.S. Government agency National Institute of Health (NIH) has launched it's own DNA tests which provide genetic information at no cost. The purpose is to have genetic sequenced data for scientific research and the benefit is having that data provided to you for free. Not everyone may feel comfortable with this, but it is a free alternative to commercial DNA tests.

Centimorgans:

Centimorgans are useful for determining how closely related you are to someone. The reference chart on the next page shows average cMs for a given relationship. Keep in mind it's usually more of a range than an absolute number. This is because genetics are somewhat random and while usually things are a 50/50 split from generation to generation the 50% of your father that you get won't be the same as the 50% your sibling gets and similarly through the generations.

Centimorgan Reference:

Parent/Child	3400	cMs
Sibling	2640	cMs
Aunt/Uncle/Niece/Nephew	1320	cMs
Half Sibling	1700	cMs
Half Aunt/Uncle/Niece/Nephew	850	cMs
Grandparent/Grandchild	1700	cMs
Aunt/Uncle	1350	cMs
1st Cousin	850	cMs
Half 1st Cousin	425	cMs
1st Cousin 1 removed	425	cMs
1st Cousin x2 removed	212	cMs
1st Cousin x3 removed	106	cMs
1st Cosuins x4 removed	53	cMs
Great Grandparent/Grandchild	850	cMs
Great Aunt/Uncle/Niece/Nephew	850	cMs
1st Cousin x1 removed	425	cMs
2nd Cousin	212	cMs
Great Great Grandparent/Grandchild	425	cMs
Great Grand Aunt/Uncle/Niece/Nephew	425	cMs
2nd Cousin x1 removed	106	cMs
3rd Cousin	53	cMs
4th Cousin	13	cMs
5th Cousin	3	cMs

Conclusion

Tracing your Cherokee roots can be a worthwhile and difficult endeavor. It can be filled with surprise discoveries, shocking results, and citizenship that lasts a lifetime. Not everyone will find what they're looking for, some will find they didn't truly know who they were but gain a better understanding of their family story. Some will find new relatives they never knew they had, sometimes even brothers or sisters living in their same town.

Finding your Cherokee roots can also delve you deep into a rich and immersive culture full of entertaining stories, forgotten heroes, and a side of American history rarely taught. I wish you the best in finding what you're looking for.

GV

Wado

Resources

OKHistory.org	Includes searchable records from the Dawes Rolls and other historical records.
Ancestry.com	Great source of various information, family tree building, and DNA testing.
FamilySearch.org	Ran by the LDS church, good for family trees and it's free!
FindAGrave.com	Genealogy through gravesites.
Archives.gov	Good for archived records such as old military records.
GEDmatch.com	You can upload DNA results to find family.
23andMe.com	DNA testing.
Cherokee.org	Official Website of the Cherokee Nation
EBCI.com	Official Website of the Eastern Band of Cherokee Indians
UKB-nsn.gov	Official Website of the UKB
BIA.gov	Bureau of Indian Affairs
VisitCherokeeNation.com	Information on the many attractions within the Cherokee Nation and downloadable forms for help with genealogy.
JoinAllOfUs.com	Free DNA Test from NIH
NCAI.org/tribal-directory	A Directory of Tribal Nations

Cherokee Syllabary

D R T ꮰ Ꭳ i Ꮝ Ꭸ Ꮖ Ꭹ A J E ꮎ Ꭾ Ꭻ

Ꮄ Ꭺ Ꮆ W ꝺ Ꮅ G M Ꭵ ꮕ Ꭱ H Ꮒ Ꭹ Ꮊ Ꮻ Ꮐ

G Ꭷ Ꮂ Z Ꭳ Ꮴ Ꮖ Ꮼ Ꮽ Ꮼ Ꮈ Ɛ Ꮼ ꮄ 4 Ꮟ

Ꮵ Ꮲ R Ꮮ W Ꮪ Ꮧ Ꭾ Ꮴ V S Ꮙ Ꮆ Ꮈ L C

Ꮗ Ꮒ P G Ꮦ Ꮵ Ꮳ K Ꮷ C G Ꮕ Ꮕ Ꮒ Ꭹ Ꮝ Ꮬ

Ꮸ Ꮬ Ꮵ Ꮒ B G

Cherokee Treaties

Pre-American Revolution

Treaty between two Cherokee towns with English traders of Carolina, 1684
Treaty with South Carolina, 1721
Treaty of Nikwasi, 1730
Treaty of Whitehall, 1730
Treaty with South Carolina, 24 November 1755
Treaty with North Carolina, 1756
Treaty of Long-Island-on-the-Holston, 20 July 1761
Treaty of Charlestown, 18 December 1761
Treaty of Johnson Hall, 12 March 1768
Treaty of Hard Labour, 14 October 1768
Treaty of Lochaber, 18 October 1770
Treaty with Virginia, early 1772
Treaty of Augusta, 1 June 1773
Treaty of Sycamore Shoals, 14 March 1775

Pre-U.S. Constitution

Treaty of Dewitt's Corner, 20 May 1777
Treaty of Fort Henry, 20 July 1777
Treaty of Long-Island-on-the-Holston, 26 July 1781
Treaty of Augusta,[3] 25 May 1783
Treaty of Long Swamp Creek, 30 May 1783
Treaty of Pensacola, 30 May 1784
Treaty of Dumplin Creek, 10 June 1785
Treaty of Hopewell, 28 November 1785
Treaty of Coyatee, 3 August 1786

Post-U.S. Constitution

Treaty of Holston, 2 July 1791
Treaty of Philadelphia, 17 February 1792
Treaty of Walnut Hills, 10 April 1792
Treaty of Pensacola, 26 September 1792
Treaty of Philadelphia, 26 June 1794
Treaty of Tellico Blockhouse, 8 November 1794
Treaty of Tellico, 2 October 1798
Treaty of Tellico, 24 October 1804
Treaty of Tellico, 25 October 1805
Treaty of Tellico, 27 October 1805
Treaty of Washington, 7 January 1806
Treaty of Fort Jackson, 9 August 1814
Treaties of Washington, 22 March 1816
Treaty of Chickasaw Council House, 14 September 1816
Map of the Treaty of the Cherokee Agency, 8 July 1817
Treaty of the Cherokee Agency, 8 July 1817
Treaty of Washington, 27 February 1819
Council Bluffs Treaty, 11 December 1821
Treaty of San Antonio de Bexar, with the Spanish Empire, 8 November 1822
Treaty of Washington, 6 May 1828
Treaty of New Echota, 29 December 1835
Treaty of Bowles Village with the Republic of Texas, 23 February 1836
Treaty of Bird's Fort with the Republic of Texas, 29 September 1843
Treaty of Tehuacana Creek with the Republic of Texas, 1844
Treaty of Washington, 6 August 1846
Treaty of Fort Smith, Arkansas, 13 September 1865
Treaty of the Cherokee Nation, 19 July 1866
Treaty of Washington, 29 April 1868

ABOUT THE AUTHOR

Joseph Reece is a Cherokee Nation citizen who has been featured on television for tracing his family back through the Trail of Tears. Joseph is also of Yu'pik, Creek, and European descent. Besides genealogy Joseph enjoys spending time with family, traveling, meeting new people, and making music (which is available on most streaming services).